Portraits of the Gateway to Wales

by M. C. Stinchcombe

Kingsmead

Kingsmead Press
Rosewell House
Kingsmead Square
Bath

0 906230 35 7

Text set in 11/13 pt VIP Palatino, printed by photolithography,
and bound in Great Britain at The Pitman Press, Bath

Contents

	Page
Abergavenny Town Hall and Market	5
Market Street	7
The Castle	9
St. Mary's Church	11
Plas Derwen	13
Llanfoist Bridge	15
Old Court	17
Victoria Street	19
Bailey Park	21
Bryntirion	23
Ross Road	25
Canal Bridge, Llanover	27
The Boathouse, Llanfoist	29
Clydach Gorge	31
Cottages at Gellifelen	33
Mill Lane, Govilon	35
St. Peter's, Llanwenarth Citra	37
Llanthony Valley	39
St. Martin's, Cwmyoy	41
Skenfrith Castle	43
Old Cottage, Treadam	45
Wernddu	47

1. Abergavenny Town Hall and Market

Abergavenny is a busy market town situated on the rivers Usk and Gavenny. It was first settled by the Romans but little remains to show the exact site, just a few coins and relics. After the conquest of 1066 the Normans arrived and established a more permanent base, building a castle at this strategic point, a natural convergence of valley routes. Sheltered by the surrounding mountains it proved to be an ideal situation and the town developed steadily.

The progress of Abergavenny can be attributed to its geographical advantages. Sheep farming on the mountains led to a flourishing wool and flannel trade while farming on the lower slopes and river meadows provided other essentials, various crops, dairy foods and meat. These brought prosperity over the years particularly at the time of the French Wars of 1789 when all these commodities were in great demand. At the time of the Industrial Revolution and the accompanying agricultural activity essential links were established with the Valley Towns with the building of the canal and railway. This made Abergavenny a natural centre for trade until the decline in the 1920s.

Although the manufacturing occupations suffered, the farming industry survived and today the Tuesday market is a big event attracting visitors from miles around. There has been a Town Hall and market place here since 1602. The present building was erected in 1794 without the tower which was added later – its copper roof forming a distinctive landmark visible from every route into the town.

2. Market Street

Market Street with its raised mediaeval pavement leads to the lower open market stalls and the cattle market opposite. This is one of the largest livestock markets in Wales and attracts custom from far and wide. In addition to the weekly markets there are regular pony sales and special stock sales, in the modern sheds and pens which have just been rebuilt.

The street was formerly known as Traitors Lane. It seems that when Owen Glendower threatened the town in 1404 a woman who supported his cause opened the gate to the invaders who proceeded to reduce the town to ashes. Owen Glendower was descended from the princes of North Wales and had been a loyal soldier to the king. However, he became a natural leader of the Welsh national uprising. There followed a period of insurrection and unrest against the English that lasted about fifteen years when his influence waned and he became an outlaw until his death in obscurity.

In these early times the narrow shop fronts would have the workroom immediately inside extending backwards with the living quarters above and cellars beneath, with the family often taking their name from their trade.

3. The Castle

Hamelyn de Baladon who came over with the Conqueror, built the castle and town wall on rising ground near the River Usk, not far from the Roman settlement of Gobannium.

The castle was built as a garrison rather than a nobleman's residence and was one of many used by the Norman Barons to subdue the Welsh over the next 200 years. These Marcher Lords were granted all the lands they could conquer, gradually driving back the Welsh and building castles to secure their gains. One of the most fearsome Lords of Abergavenny was William de Braose who committed many atrocities, until after many changes the Lordship passed to the Nevill family in 1417. By this time the need for maintaining the castle had disappeared and it had fallen into disrepair. Today what little remains has been well preserved and houses the town's Museum.

Traces of the town wall are still visible. It originally enclosed an area of about twenty acres with the community living in wooden houses.

4. St. Mary's Church

The parish church stands on the site of the Priory which was built by Hamelyn just outside the town wall, but nothing remains of the original priory and very little of the Norman church. After the Dissolution of the monasteries by Henry VIII the site was bought by the town burgesses who built a new large parish church to replace the older and smaller St. John's. Since then the building has been extensively restored but the monuments inside bear witness to its age, many of them older than the church itself – the oldest tomb bearing the date 1273. Particularly interesting is the carved wooden figure of Jesse with a tree issuing from his body, a rare example of its kind.

The original parish church of St. John's with its ivy-covered tower was then used for the Grammar School which King Henry VIII founded in 1542 and which is now in modern buildings overlooking the town.

5. Plas Derwen

The Welsh name means Oak Tree Mansion. It is known to be very old dated about the 15th century. One of the inside walls is 5 feet 6 inches thick which suggests that the house was built around an old structure. Upstairs is a leper's room – the door has a covered peep-hole in it, both of which can only be opened from the inside. There is a large wooded garden with a stream from the Little Skirrid flowing through which is culverted under the house, it is possible to see from one end to the other. The stream passes under the road and eventually joins the Usk.

Like so many older houses it has been altered and enlarged by subsequent owners and its origins lost in the past.

6. Llanfoist Bridge

Remains of what may have been old piers suggest that an earlier bridge crossed the Usk at a point just below the Castle. Here at Llanfoist a bridge with sixteen arches was constructed in Tudor times but it was rather low and subject to flooding. It was later raised and altered then again in more recent times when further modifications took place leaving it as it stands today – with eight arches, all apparently different. A second bridge was constructed alongside in the early 1800s to carry the tramway to Abergavenny and later still Brunel's steam railway but it was demolished a few years ago after the closure of the line.

The Usk rises in the Black Mountains to the west of Brecon. Its tributary, the Gavenny, draws its water from the Sugar Loaf and the Skirrid. The town stretch is fished extensively for salmon and trout, while further downstream the nearby golf course offers different sport in an equally ideal setting.

7. Old Court

This house was built in the sixteenth century and was known as Beili Baker, being the home of many generations of the Baker family who were stewards to the Lords of Abergavenny. That line became extinct but was then represented by the Gabb family through marriage, both families playing a prominent role in the life of the town.

It was built on the old town wall and was adjacent to the Tudor, or West, Gate of which the town had four. The town wall continued on the other side of Tudor Street behind the King's Arms and the houses in Nevill Street, where it is still visible. The gate was standing until 1802.

There are virtually no traces of buildings before Tudor times due to the ravages of Owen Glendower. The first Tudor king was Henry VII who had spent his boyhood with his Uncle, Jasper Tudor, at Pembroke Castle. On his Accession in 1485 he gave Jasper the task of rebuilding Abergavenny – the next Tudor king, Henry VIII, granted the first Charter in 1542.

8. Victoria Street

In 1794 Lawyer Baker Gabb became the owner of the Grofields which had been part of the Beili Baker estate. Grofield, meaning high or big, was the high meadow to the west of the town where cattle were "empastured" when the castle meadows flooded. A licence to build was granted at the beginning of the following century at the time of the Industrial Revolution when workers' cottages were needed. Several fields were built on and named Victoria Street, Regent Street, Princes Street, Baker Street, etc., while the Railway provided cottages for their workers, namely, Stanhope Street, Commercial Road, and Junction Cottages.

Whilst new areas were being developed older parts were demolished and rebuilt. The Georgian houses in Nevill Street were erected in Regency times to provide elegant town houses for the professional men – lawyers, doctors, etc. – leaving properties like the Cow Inn on the opposite side of the road untouched.

This was the beginning of a period of rapid growth which saw the population almost quadrupled by the end of the nineteenth century.

9. Bailey Park

Crawshay Bailey, who was a local ironmaster, gave the land to the town in 1884 for the creation of a park. He was a man of character and enterprise successfully developing industries at Nantyglo, Merthyr Tydfil and elsewhere. Some ironmasters were harsh but others were benefactors providing houses, schools, recreation places, and giving pensions to those workers who were blinded. Crawshay Bailey played an important part in the life of the time – he was several times M.P. for Monmouth – and is buried at Llanfoist in the church he helped to restore.

Today the park plays a vital role in the town with its recreational facilities, the swimming pool, bowling green, tennis courts and pitches. Its chief attraction must be the beautiful setting with the views of the surrounding mountains, the variety of mature trees, and the well kept gardens.

10. Bryntirion

This house was erected about 1860 being one of a wide variety of styles built with the soft grey local stone. The mountains around the town are: the Sugar Loaf with its three shoulders Llanwenarth Breast, Rholben and Deri; Great Skirrid or Holy Mountain; Little Skirrid; and the Blorenge which is the commencement of the coal and iron-bearing range that extends westwards to the Brecon Beacons. It was from quarries on the Deri and Blorenge as well as nearby Clydach and Llanfihangel that Abergavenny obtained its stone. It is seen throughout the district and used for all kinds of construction.

Blasting for stone still continues at Clydach sending a cloud of dust and noise reverberating round the hills. Quarries elsewhere have mostly closed allowing the scars to heal over leaving barely discernible signs of their existence. The mountains have returned to their natural beauty and peace so much appreciated by the walker.

11. Ross Road

Abergavenny has grown up over the years with a bewildering variety of architecture and material. At different stages of development there have been corresponding changes in requirements. This has led to an intermingling of age and style with neither one dominating the other. It is this lack of conformity which gives the town its visual appeal. This row of attractive cottages was obviously built as one unit but a glance at the roof-line in any of the main streets, the shopping area in particular, will demonstrate the individual choice that has gone into each and every structure.

Alterations to the roads into the town had a lot to do with the changing appearance. When the new roads were established in the 1830s many of the older quarters became by-passed leaving them unaffected by modern trends.

12. Canal Bridge, Llanover

This is just one of the one hundred and sixty six bridges over the Monmouthshire and Brecon Canal, which was commenced at Brecon in 1795 and completed in stages to reach Newport in 1818. The canal was built on the contour of the mountains which enabled barges easy navigation as there were few locks to negotiate. It also meant that it took many twists and turns giving ever-changing views across the magnificent countryside. As well as the bridges carrying roads over the canal there are also several small aqueducts carrying the canal over the road giving very shallow clearance.

The canal was constructed to carry goods from numerous ironworks and coalmines in the two counties. A large amount of trade was done for many years, but its usefulness lessened as the railway spread leaving the canal obsolete. It is used now for pleasure boating, fishing and walking for as a great deal of its length is within the National Park area it has assumed a different role.

Although its use has changed water is still supplied to a local steelworks at the rate of four million gallons a day. The canal is fed by streams from the mountains which support it, the level being controlled by "plugs" which can be pulled to release any excess.

13. The Boathouse, Llanfoist

Llanfoist is situated on the southern side of the river from Abergavenny, sheltered by the steep wooded slopes of the Blorenge. The canal reached here about 1801 and runs just above the village through the trees. The wharves and bridges along its length now offer facilities for the pleasure craft and give access to all the countryside around. There are few locks to negotiate although on the stretch between here and Brecon there is a tunnel where boats have to use their headlights.

As the building of the canal progressed tramways were built from the mines to the wharves which were the link between road, rail, and water. These tramways consisted of narrow gauge track with small wagons pulled by horses or mules.

The Boathouse was originally an iron-warehouse built by the Blaenavon Iron Company at the end of their tramway. This ran down the side of the Blorenge from their works to the wharf at Llanfoist. From there goods would be transported by canal, or by tramway which reached as far as Hereford.

14. Clydach Gorge

Clydach Gorge with its steep sides and fast flowing river is the only natural entry into the industrial valleys from the Usk valley. Some three miles in length it bears comparison with any other similar location. Its wild rugged beauty must have been even more impressive before the advent of road and rail. From the north it gives access to the heads of the iron- and coal-bearing valleys which run in a southerly direction towards the coast of Wales. When the mineral wealth was exploited the area was found to have the four ingredients essential to success – trees, ironstone, limestone, and water. Among the busy industrial Valley Towns there are still traces of what must have been country of outstanding scenic beauty.

Within the boundary of the Brecon Beacons National Park the Clydach valley has remained relatively unspoilt. The roadway came up here crossing the mountains and joining all the valleys. Today it is superseded by the modern three-lane Heads of the Valleys Road which was completed in the early 1960s going from Abergavenny to Hirwaun, a distance of about thirty miles.

The railway came through in 1854 taking over from the tramways which had served the mining towns between Abergavenny and Dowlais, where was the largest ironworks in South Wales. The railway closed in 1958 but the line can still be seen, with a roadway above it, clinging to the side of the mountain – a remarkable feat of engineering.

15. Cottages at Gellifelen

Like many others in the district these cottages on top of the mountain are now derelict due to the closure of the mines. They were typical miners dwellings with two up and two down, a lean-to kitchen and a shared privvy, with steep roofs to dispel the heavy falls of rain and snow. While the inhabitants enjoyed full employment and prosperity there was little hardship but in bad times the larger communities managed to keep going but the more isolated places suffered. The young people would move away to find work and some social amenities leaving the older ones behind. The properties eventually became empty and fell into decay. The weather too played a part in this migration, it can be very bleak on top and day to day living even in the best of times would be very demanding, in adverse conditions of employment it would seem to have no reason.

16. Mill Lane, Govilon

Although only a few hundred yards from the Heads of the Valleys Road Govilon has remained unspoilt and retains its old world charm. It is a village of rambling lanes lying at the side of the Blorenge with magnificent views of the mountains and the valley of the Usk. The mill is now derelict but the cottages in the narrow lane are well cared for.

The village has always been well populated due to the many limestone quarries in the vicinity. The name Govilon comes from the Welsh name for forge indicating the existence here of early ironworks long before the Industrial Revolution. The nearby hamlet of Pwlldu which lies high up the cwm behind Govilon did not survive the regression and is mostly ruinous.

Here again at Govilon is the junction of road, rail, and water, but while the railway no longer exists the wharf on the canal has provided the ideal situation for a thriving boat club.

Govilon used to be part of the large parish of Llanwenarth, housing the major portion of the population which would commute across the Usk by ferry to Llanwenarth which lies only one mile from Abergavenny.

17. St. Peter's, Llanwenarth Citra

The present building was erected about 1631 but there has been a church on this site since the sixth century. The parish was very large and divided by the River Usk into Llanwenarth Citra, "this side" of the river and Llanwenarth Ultra, "the other", or southern side. Whilst the church has always been on this side, the population has mainly been on the other and was provided with a halfpenny ferry by the Church who collected the revenue. It was running as recently as the early 1950s.

The parish split in 1860 when Llanwenarth Ultra was taken into the parish of Govilon and in 1957 Llanwenarth Citra was grouped with St. Mary's Church in Abergavenny. Most of the parish on the northern side is open mountain, the highest point being the Sugar Loaf, Mynydd Pen-y-Fal, at 1,955 feet above sea level, and is within the boundary of the Brecon Beacons National Park.

18. Llanthony Valley

For enjoyment of Nature in all her aspects, set in the heart
of the Black Mountains, this valley is renowned for its
unspoilt beauty. It must have attracted the Normans who
established a Priory here in 1103 on the site of a sixth
century chapel of St. David. The Normans preferred to
build in secluded spots on the banks of a river, in this
instance the Honddu. By the time of the Dissolution the
Priory was already declining as some of the Monks had
moved to new premises in Gloucester which proved more
popular. The ruins are quite extensive with parts of the
infirmary and chapel incorporated into the village church.

Further up the valley is Capel-y-ffin where Father
Ignatius established a small community in 1870. With only
a few scattered farms along its length the valley culminates
in the Gospel Pass presenting a spectacular view from the
Hay Bluff.

19. St. Martin's, Cwmyoy

Cwmyoy is a small village scattered under the slopes of Hatterall Hill at the beginning of the Llanthony Valley whose northern heights are a boundary of the National Park. The church is ancient and at some time in its long history has suffered from a landslip which has twisted the foundations. There seems to be no part which is at right-angles to any other, nothing is in alignment. Although this presents a very unstable appearance the church stands firm. Its age is undetermined but dates back to mediaeval times, the oak woodwork inside is of the seventeenth century. St. Martin's, with the churches at Llanthony and Oldcastle used to be in the diocese of Hereford but since 1844 have been included in that of Llandaff.

There are several of these historical Black Mountain churches within a comparatively small area, all long established, probably originating as chapels on the pilgrim routes to Llanthony. Many have been sited in obscure positions difficult of access, Partrishow church in the neighbouring Grwyne Fawr valley can only be reached on foot.

20. Skenfrith Castle

This is the smallest of the "Trilateral" group which included the adjacent fortresses of White and Grosmont. They came under the same Lordship and were at one time commanded by three brothers. Both White Castle and Grosmont Castle were moated strongholds on hill-top sites with dominating views of the surrounding countryside, while Skenfrith Castle occupied a low-lying position on the River Monnow. It was built in the thirteenth century and is one of the earliest of the many Border castles – there were about twenty-five in Monmouthshire alone, the most imposing being Raglan – but many of the sites have been lost.

The church of St. Bridget in the small village that grew up around the castle has walls five feet thick as it would also have been a place of refuge. It has a lantern, or dovecot, tower – the most perfect example of its kind.

21. Old Cottage, Treadam

Dated circa 1600 this beautiful stone cottage seems to have taken root and become as one with its environment. The Elizabethan chamferings and stone staircase place it between 1560 and 1600. It is thought the Reeve of White Castle (one mile away) may have lived here; at this time the castle was used solely as an administration centre for local affairs. The castles of the Trilateral were about five miles from each other but White Castle became the most prominent as a military garrison. It was immensely strengthened in the thirteenth century at the time of great unrest along the marches when the Normans were trying to subdue the Welsh. It is the best preserved of the border castles due to its splendid stonework.

Unlike Grosmont and Skenfrith no village grew up around its imposing walls. After its usefulness as a fortification it became disused and finally derelict whilst nearby Old Cottage remains intact and unaltered after nearly four hundred years.

22. Wernddu

Wernddu is reputedly the oldest house in the county. It was built in the twelfth century with strong foundations and thick stone walls which supported a stone roof weighing about sixty tons. It shows little sign of its great antiquity as over the centuries there have been many alterations by successive owners. Inside there is a very fine wooden staircase carved in the 1600s, which has survived through following generations.

Coaches passed this way between the Angel Hotel in Abergavenny and the town of Ross some 24 miles away, until the owner at that time took exception to the traffic rumbling by. He had the road diverted away from his property which left the nearby village of Bryn-y-Gwenin a cul-de-sac.

In early times Wernddu was the only house between Monmouth and Abergavenny. Until just over one hundred years ago it was the seat of the eldest branch of the Herbert family which under various surnames has spread into nearly every county of the Principality.

The Public Library, Abergavenny